THIS NOTEBOOK
BELONGS TO

ANNUAL LEAVE

BECAUSE HOLIDAY SOUNDS LIKE TOO MUCH FUN

NOTES

BACKFILL

REPLACING SOMEONE WHO HAS BEEN

SACKED/RESIGNED/DIED

NOTES

BENCHMARKING

MEASURING

NOTES

BIO-BREAK

USE THE TOILET/HAVE A LITTLE CRY

NOTES

BLAMESTORMING

DECIDING WHICH PERSON OR DEPARTMENT TO BLAME FOR THE
LATEST BALLS UP

NOTES

BLEEDING EDGE

BECAUSE CUTTING EDGE ISN'T CUTTING EDGE ENOUGH

NOTES

BLUE SKY THINKING
COMING UP WITH "UNACTIONABLE" IDEAS

NOTES

BOTTOM OUT

GRIN AND BEAR IT TILL IT GETS BETTER

NOTES

CAPACITY

ABILITY

NOTES

CASCADE THIS DOWN

PASS ON INFORMATION TO YOUR CO-WORKERS

NOTES

CHANGE MANAGEMENT

NEW MANAGERS THAT WILL CHANGE A COMPANY, USUALLY
INTO A SMALLER ONE IE. SACK SOME PEOPLE

NOTES

CLOSE OF PLAY

HOME TIME

NOTES

DELIVERABLES

THINGS YOU ARE/WERE SUPPOSED TO DO

NOTES

DRILL DOWN

LOOK AT SOMETHING IN DETAIL

NOTES

DUCKS IN A ROW, GET OUR
TO ORGANISE

NOTES

FLAGPOLE, RUN THIS UP THE

TRY IT OUT

NOTES

GOING FORWARD
FROM NOW ON

NOTES

GUERRILLA EDIT

WORKING ON YOUR PART OF A PROJECT WHILE SOMEONE ELSE WORKS ON THEIR PART OF THE PROJECT

NOTES

HELICOPTER VIEW

LOOK AT SOMETHING ON A LARGE SCALE

NOTES

HUMAN CAPITAL
THE VALUE OF A PERSON

NOTES

HYPERVISING

LIKE SUPERVISING BUT MUCH CLEVERER, IMPORTANT AND PRETENTIOUS

NOTES

INBOX ME

EMAIL ME

NOTES

INTERFACE
TALK TO EACH OTHER

NOTES

INCENTIVIZE
MOTIVATE

NOTES

KEY
IMPORTANT

NOTES

LEARNINGS

LESSONS

NOTES

LEVERAGE
EXPLOIT/USE

NOTES

MATRIX

AN ORGANIZATIONAL STRUCTURE THAT USUALLY MEANS YOU HAVE MULTIPLE MANAGERS/HOOPS TO JUMP THROUGH

NOTES

MISSION

A MORE MACHO WAY OF SAYING TASK

NOTES

MONETIZING
MAKING MONEY FROM

NOTES

MOOFING, I AM
MOBILE AND OUT OF THE OFFICE

NOTES

NO-BRAINER, ITS A

I HAVE COME UP WITH AN AMAZING IDEA, JUST GO
ALONG WITH IT

NOTES

NURTURE BUBBLE

AN INVISIBLE AND IMAGINARY FORCE FIELD THAT IS SUPPOSED
TO KEEP OUT CRITICISM

NOTES

OPEN THE KIMONO

SHARE INFORMATION

NOTES

PARADIGM SHIFT

BIG CHANGE

NOTES

PRODUCTIZE

TURN SOMETHING INTO A PRODUCT

NOTES

PUSH THE ENVELOPE
TO TRY SOMETHING THAT'S NEVER BEEN DONE
(USUALLY FOR A GOOD REASON)

NOTES

REPURPOSING

RECYCLING

NOTES

RESIZING

FIRING SOME PEOPLE

NOTES

RIGHTSHORING

OR "OUTSOURCING" GIVING YOUR JOB TO AN OVERSEAS
WORKER FOR A FRACTION OF THE PAY

NOTES

RINGFENCE

PROTECT

NOTES

ROBUST

HEALTHY

NOTES

SCOPE CREEP
CHANGING THE BRIEF AS A PROJECT PROGRESSES

NOTES

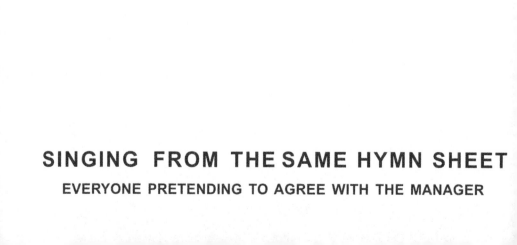

SINGING FROM THE SAME HYMN SHEET

EVERYONE PRETENDING TO AGREE WITH THE MANAGER

NOTES

SOUP TO NUTS, FROM
START TO FINISH

NOTES

SYNERGIZE

COOPERATE

NOTES

TAKEAWAY

THE ONE THING YOU SHOULD REMEMBER FROM A MEETING

NOTES

THOUGHT SHOWER

BECAUSE BRAINSTORMING IS NOW OFFENSIVE
TO EPILEPTICS

NOTES

TOUCH BASE

TO CONTACT SOMEONE

NOTES

TRANSITION

TO SACK, FIRE, GIVE THE BOOT

NOTES

UPLIFT
TO GET OR ACQUIRE

NOTES

UP-SKILLING

A WAY OF GETTING MORE WORK OUT OF ONE PERSON FOR THE SAME PAY

NOTES

ZERO TASKING
A COOL WAY OF DOING NOTHING

NOTES

CORPORATE **JARGON** BINGO

BLUE-SKY THINKING	ITS ON MY RADAR	TOUCH BASE
RE-INVENT THE WHEEL	VALUE ADDED	HIT THE GROUND RUNNING
CIRCLE BACK	DRILL DOWN	NO BRAINER
TACKLE THAT HEAD ON	CLOSE OF PLAY	PROACTIVE

CORPORATE JARGON BINGO

BLUE-SKY THINKING	ITS ON MY RADAR	TOUCH BASE
RE-INVENT THE WHEEL	VALUE ADDED	HIT THE GROUND RUNNING
CIRCLE BACK	DRILL DOWN	NO BRAINER
TACKLE THAT HEAD ON	CLOSE OF PLAY	PROACTIVE

CORPORATE JARGON BINGO

BLUE-SKY THINKING	ITS ON MY RADAR	TOUCH BASE
RE-INVENT THE WHEEL	VALUE ADDED	HIT THE GROUND RUNNING
CIRCLE BACK	DRILL DOWN	NO BRAINER
TACKLE THAT HEAD ON	CLOSE OF PLAY	PROACTIVE

CORPORATE **JARGON** BINGO

BLUE-SKY THINKING	ITS ON MY RADAR	TOUCH BASE
RE-INVENT THE WHEEL	VALUE ADDED	HIT THE GROUND RUNNING
CIRCLE BACK	DRILL DOWN	NO BRAINER
TACKLE THAT HEAD ON	CLOSE OF PLAY	PROACTIVE

CORPORATE **JARGON** BINGO

BLUE-SKY THINKING	ITS ON MY RADAR	TOUCH BASE
RE-INVENT THE WHEEL	VALUE ADDED	HIT THE GROUND RUNNING
CIRCLE BACK	DRILL DOWN	NO BRAINER
TACKLE THAT HEAD ON	CLOSE OF PLAY	PROACTIVE

CORPORATE JARGON BINGO

BLUE-SKY THINKING	ITS ON MY RADAR	TOUCH BASE
RE-INVENT THE WHEEL	VALUE ADDED	HIT THE GROUND RUNNING
CIRCLE BACK	DRILL DOWN	NO BRAINER
TACKLE THAT HEAD ON	CLOSE OF PLAY	PROACTIVE

CORPORATE **JARGON** BINGO

BLUE-SKY THINKING	ITS ON MY RADAR	TOUCH BASE
RE-INVENT THE WHEEL	VALUE ADDED	HIT THE GROUND RUNNING
CIRCLE BACK	DRILL DOWN	NO BRAINER
TACKLE THAT HEAD ON	CLOSE OF PLAY	PROACTIVE

CORPORATE JARGON BINGO

BLUE-SKY THINKING	ITS ON MY RADAR	TOUCH BASE
RE-INVENT THE WHEEL	VALUE ADDED	HIT THE GROUND RUNNING
CIRCLE BACK	DRILL DOWN	NO BRAINER
TACKLE THAT HEAD ON	CLOSE OF PLAY	PROACTIVE

CORPORATE JARGON BINGO

BLUE-SKY THINKING	ITS ON MY RADAR	TOUCH BASE
RE-INVENT THE WHEEL	VALUE ADDED	HIT THE GROUND RUNNING
CIRCLE BACK	DRILL DOWN	NO BRAINER
TACKLE THAT HEAD ON	CLOSE OF PLAY	PROACTIVE

CORPORATE **JARGON** BINGO

BLUE-SKY THINKING	ITS ON MY RADAR	TOUCH BASE
RE-INVENT THE WHEEL	VALUE ADDED	HIT THE GROUND RUNNING
CIRCLE BACK	DRILL DOWN	NO BRAINER
TACKLE THAT HEAD ON	CLOSE OF PLAY	PROACTIVE

Positive reviews from awesome customers like you help others to feel confident about choosing Glyn Dent Books. If you have enjoyed this notebook could you take 60 seconds to go to Amazon and share your happy experiences?

I will be genuinely grateful. Thank you in advance for helping me out!

Made in the USA
Las Vegas, NV
26 June 2023

73924158R00066